CREATIVE COLOURING FOR GROWN-UPS

Pretty Patterns

Michael O'Mara Books Limited

First published in Great Britain in 2014 by
Michael O'Mara Books Limited
9 Lion Yard
Tremadoc Road
London SW4 7NQ

A CIP catalogue record for this book is available from the British Library.

Papers used by Michael O'Mara Books Limited are natural, recyclable products
made from wood grown in sustainable forests. The manufacturing processes
conform to the environmental regulations of the country of origin.

ISBN: 978-1-78243-226-5

3 4 5 6 7 8 9 10

www.mombooks.com

www.shutterstock.com with thanks to Hannah Davies for her original artworks

Designed by Billy Waqar & Claire Cater

Printed and bound in China

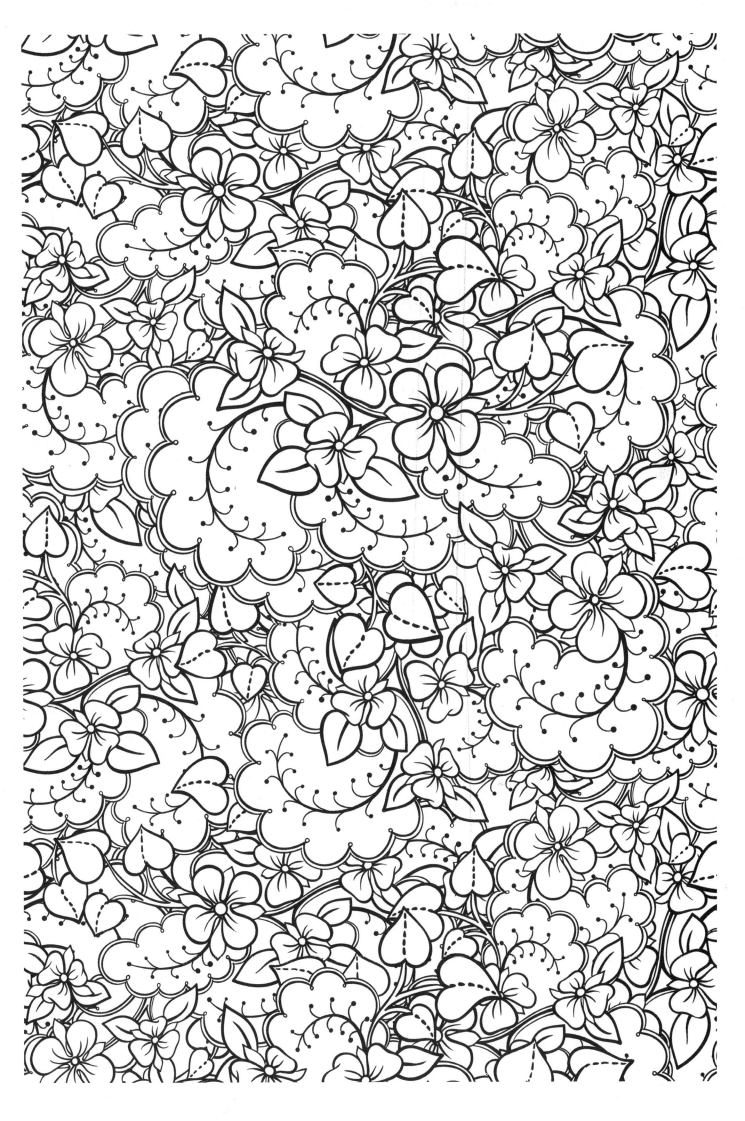

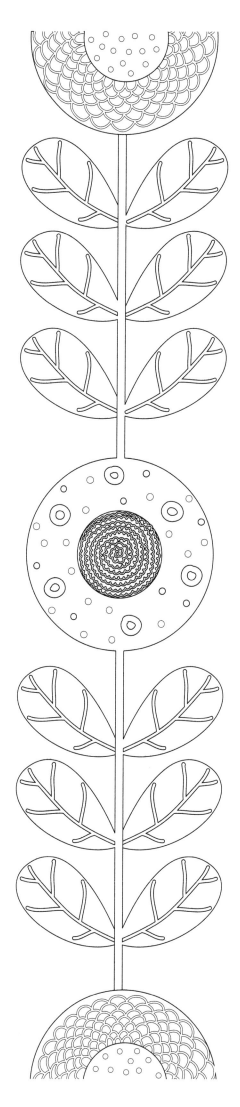